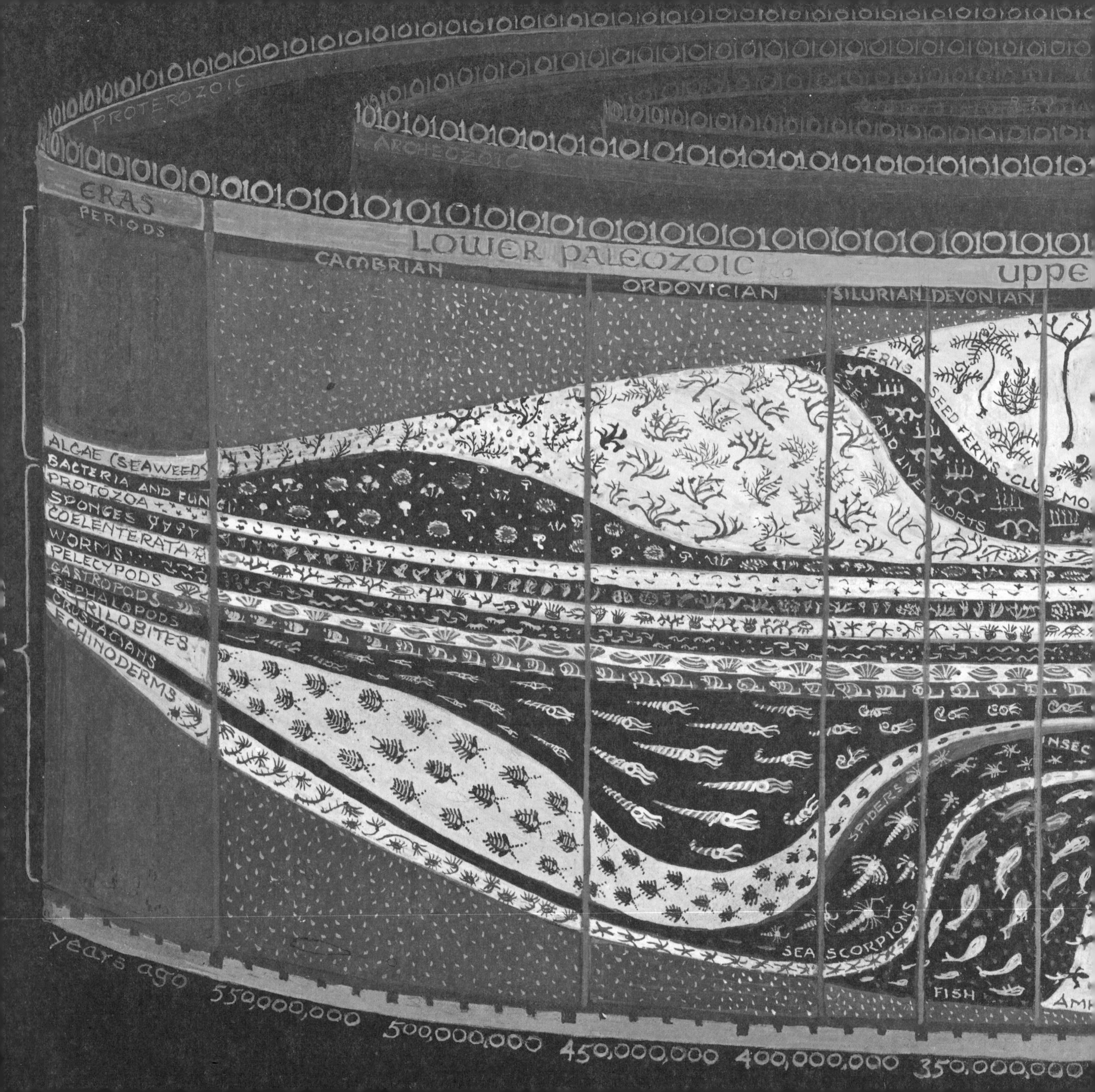

ERAS
PERIODS

PROTEROZOIC
ARCHEOZOIC

LOWER PALEOZOIC
UPPE

CAMBRIAN
ORDOVICIAN
SILURIAN DEVONIAN

FERNS
SEED FERNS · CLUB MO

ALGAE (SEAWEED)
BACTERIA AND FUNGI
PROTOZOA +
SPONGES
COELENTERATA
WORMS
PELECYPODS
GASTROPODS
CEPHALOPODS
TRILOBITES
CRUSTACIANS
ECHINODERMS

SPIDERS

INSEC

SEA SCORPIONS

FISH
AMP

years ago   550,000,000   500,000,000   450,000,000   400,000,000   350,000,000

CENOZOIC

TERTIARY

MESOZOIC

...OZOIC

PERMIAN | TRIASSIC | JURASSIC | CRETACEOUS

GYMNOSPERMS

ANGIOSPERMS

FLOWERING PLANTS

CONIFERS

CYCADS AND GINKOS

...AILS

REPTILES

DINOSAURS

BIRDS

MAMMALS

1

50,000,000

100,000,000

150,000,000

200,000,000

250,000,000

...000

ICE AGE ABOUT 1,000,000 YEARS AGO
AGE OF MAN ABOUT 25,000 YEARS

LIFE STORY
BY
VIRGINIA LEE BURTON
produced by houghton mifflin and company 1962
A PLAY IN FIVE ACTS

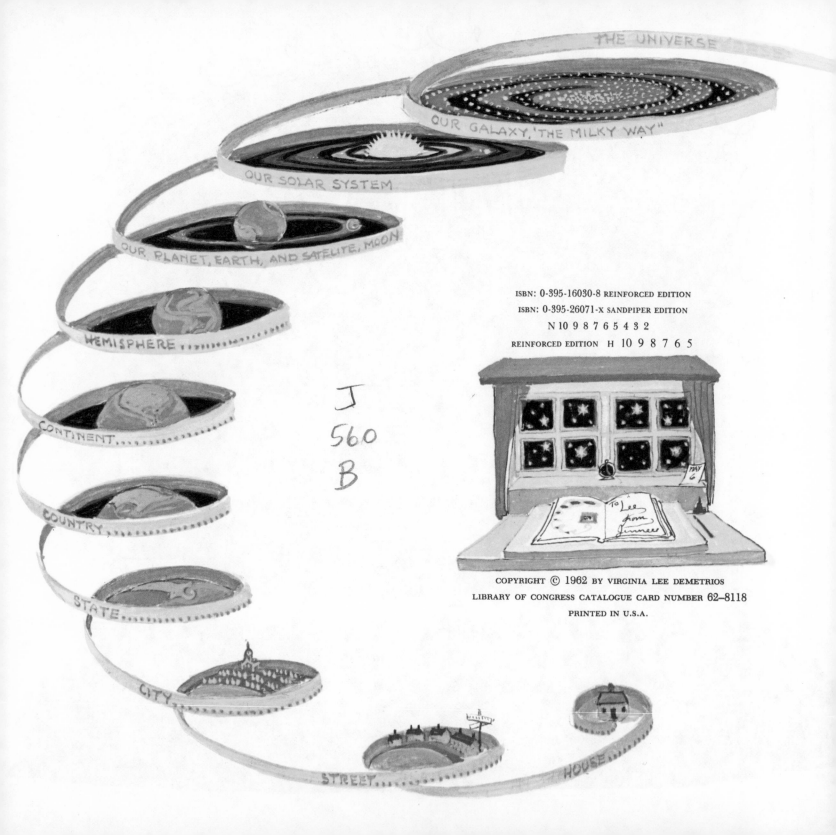

THE UNIVERSE

OUR GALAXY, "THE MILKY WAY"

OUR SOLAR SYSTEM

OUR PLANET, EARTH, AND SATELITE, MOON

HEMISPHERE

CONTINENT

COUNTRY

STATE

CITY

STREET

HOUSE

J
560
B

ISBN: 0-395-16030-8 REINFORCED EDITION

ISBN: 0-395-26071-X SANDPIPER EDITION

N 10 9 8 7 6 5 4 3 2

REINFORCED EDITION H 10 9 8 7 6 5

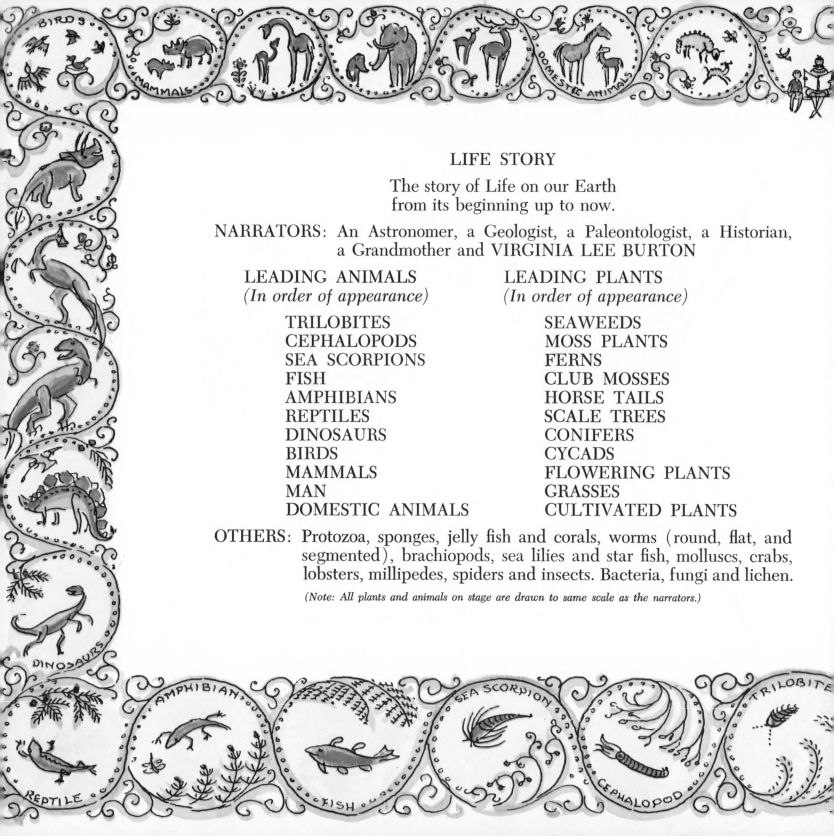

LIFE STORY

The story of Life on our Earth
from its beginning up to now.

NARRATORS: An Astronomer, a Geologist, a Paleontologist, a Historian,
a Grandmother and VIRGINIA LEE BURTON

LEADING ANIMALS
(In order of appearance)

LEADING PLANTS
(In order of appearance)

LEADING ANIMALS	LEADING PLANTS
TRILOBITES	SEAWEEDS
CEPHALOPODS	MOSS PLANTS
SEA SCORPIONS	FERNS
FISH	CLUB MOSSES
AMPHIBIANS	HORSE TAILS
REPTILES	SCALE TREES
DINOSAURS	CONIFERS
BIRDS	CYCADS
MAMMALS	FLOWERING PLANTS
MAN	GRASSES
DOMESTIC ANIMALS	CULTIVATED PLANTS

OTHERS: Protozoa, sponges, jelly fish and corals, worms (round, flat, and
segmented), brachiopods, sea lilies and star fish, molluscs, crabs,
lobsters, millipedes, spiders and insects. Bacteria, fungi and lichen.

(Note: All plants and animals on stage are drawn to same scale as the narrators.)

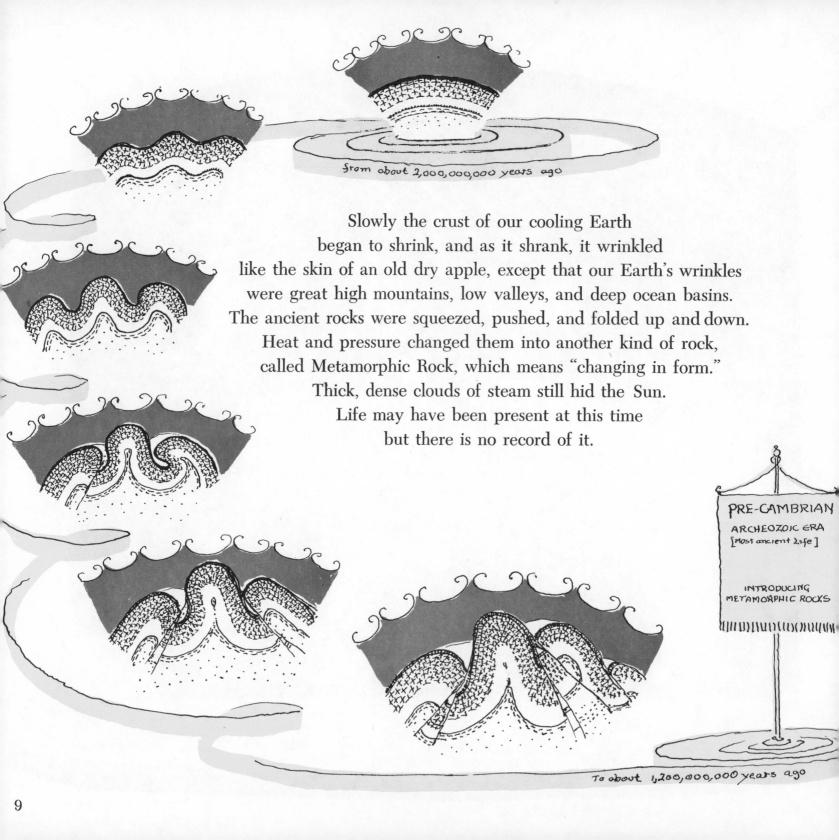

from about 2,000,000,000 years ago

Slowly the crust of our cooling Earth
began to shrink, and as it shrank, it wrinkled
like the skin of an old dry apple, except that our Earth's wrinkles
were great high mountains, low valleys, and deep ocean basins.
The ancient rocks were squeezed, pushed, and folded up and down.
Heat and pressure changed them into another kind of rock,
called Metamorphic Rock, which means "changing in form."
Thick, dense clouds of steam still hid the Sun.
Life may have been present at this time
but there is no record of it.

PRE-CAMBRIAN

ARCHEOZOIC ERA
[most ancient life]

INTRODUCING
METAMORPHIC ROCKS

To about 1,200,000,000 years ago

from about 1,200,000,000 years ago

The clouds opened —
Rain poured down in torrents
on the now cooled surface of our Earth,
filling the ocean basins and wearing down the mountains.
Rivers and streams carried little particles of rock down
and deposited them in layers on the floors of the oceans.
In time, these layers of sand, gravel, and clay
hardened into rock, called Sedimentary Rock.
It is believed that Life was present
at this time but there is little,
if any, record of it.

PRE-CAMBRIAN

PROTEROZOIC ERA
[Early Life]

INTRODUCING
SEDIMENTARY ROCKS

to about 550,000,000 years ago

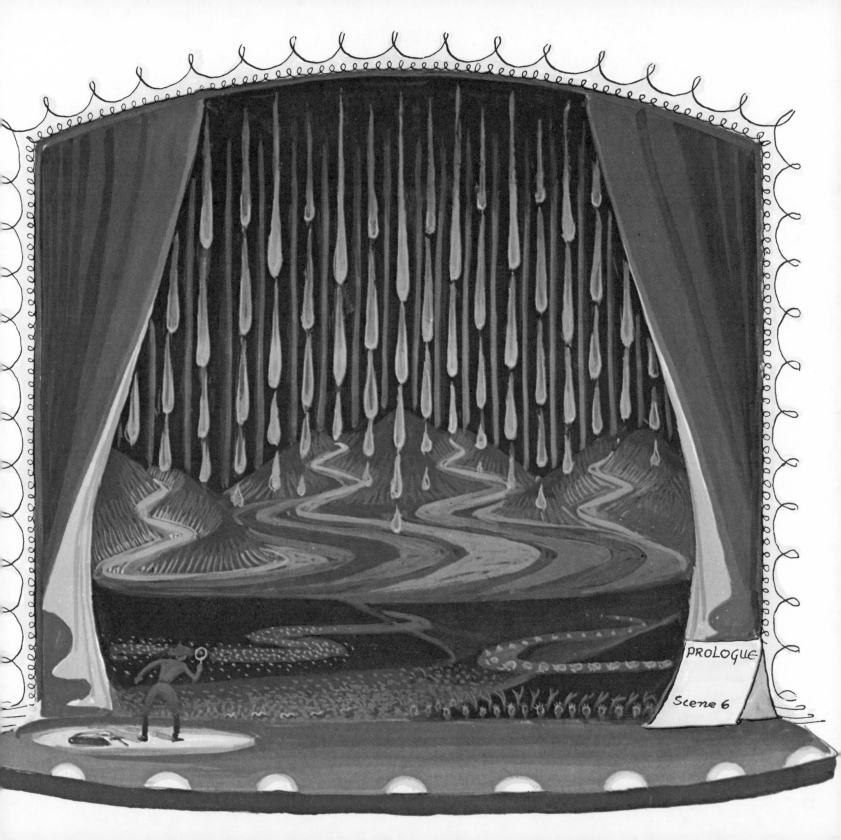

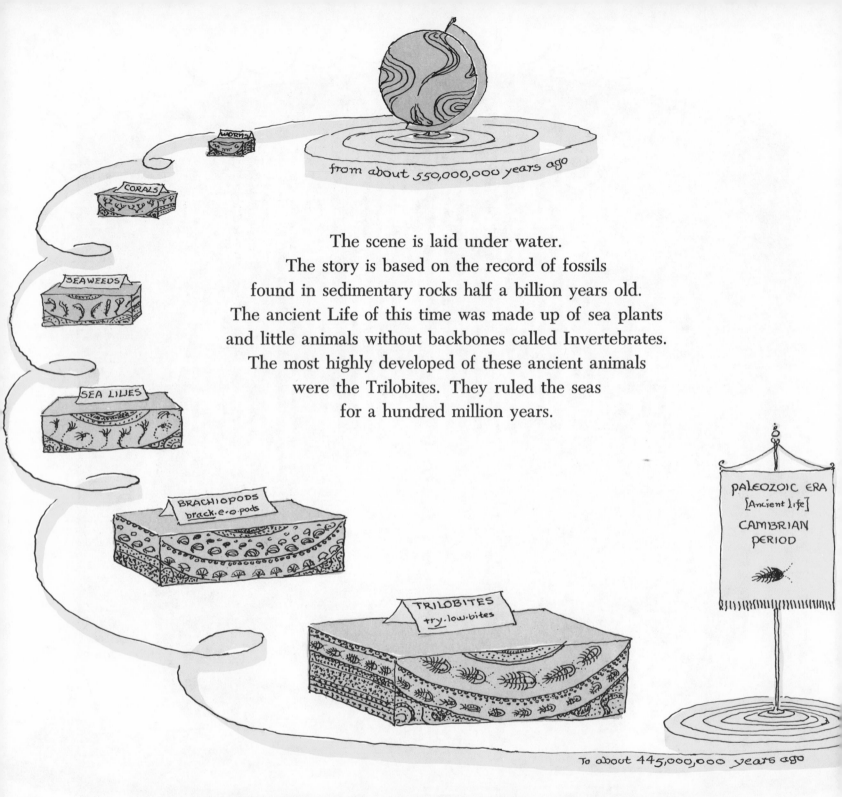

from about 550,000,000 years ago

The scene is laid under water.
The story is based on the record of fossils
found in sedimentary rocks half a billion years old.
The ancient Life of this time was made up of sea plants
and little animals without backbones called Invertebrates.
The most highly developed of these ancient animals
were the Trilobites. They ruled the seas
for a hundred million years.

WORMS

CORALS

SEAWEEDS

SEA LILIES

BRACHIOPODS
brack·e·o·pods

TRILOBITES
try·low·bites

PALEOZOIC ERA
[Ancient Life]
CAMBRIAN
PERIOD

To about 445,000,000 years ago

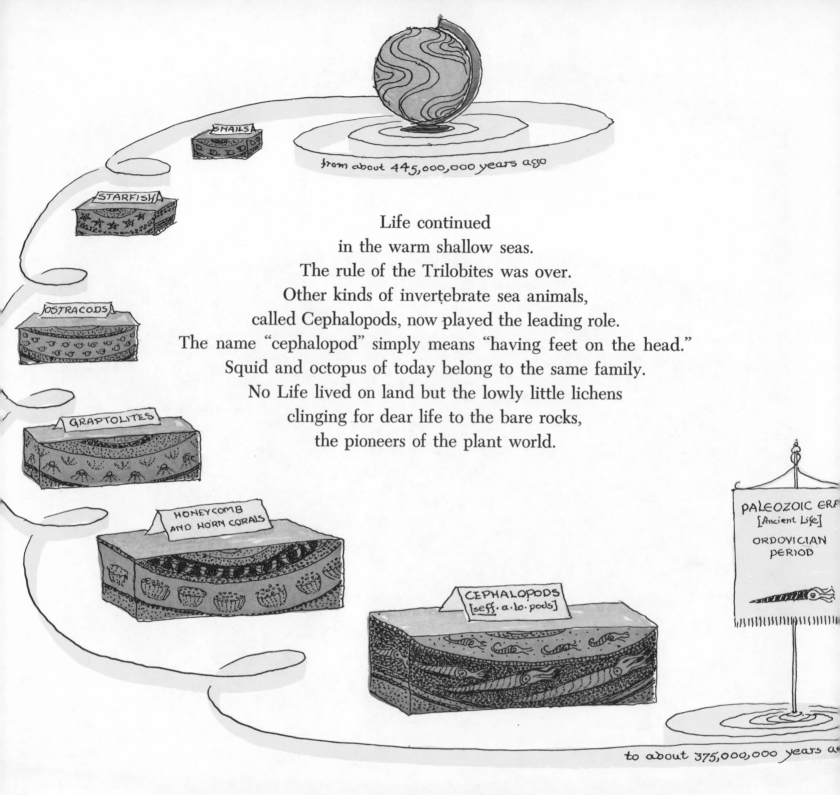

from about 445,000,000 years ago

Life continued
in the warm shallow seas.
The rule of the Trilobites was over.
Other kinds of invertebrate sea animals,
called Cephalopods, now played the leading role.
The name "cephalopod" simply means "having feet on the head."
Squid and octopus of today belong to the same family.
No Life lived on land but the lowly little lichens
clinging for dear life to the bare rocks,
the pioneers of the plant world.

SNAILS

STARFISH

OSTRACODS

GRAPTOLITES

HONEYCOMB
AND HORN CORALS

CEPHALOPODS
[seff·a·lo·pods]

PALEOZOIC ERA
[Ancient Life]

ORDOVICIAN
PERIOD

to about 375,000,000 years a

MOSSES

from about 375,000,000 years ago

LIVERWORTS

LAND SCORPIONS
AND MILLIPEDES

The scene changed as the land slowly rose.
The seas retreated or evaporated, leaving salt deposits.
A few of the water plants left high and dry became land plants—
the ancestors of the liverworts and the mosses of today.
The cephalopods had decreased in size and in number.
Sea Scorpions had taken over the rule of the seas.
Little jawless fish appeared on the scene—
the first animals to have backbones,
called Vertebrates.

JAWLESS AND
ARMORED FISH

EURYPTERIDS
[you·rip·ter·ids]
OR
SEA SCORPIONS

PALEOZOIC ERA
[Ancient Life]
SILURIAN
PERIOD

to about 350,000,000 years ago

17

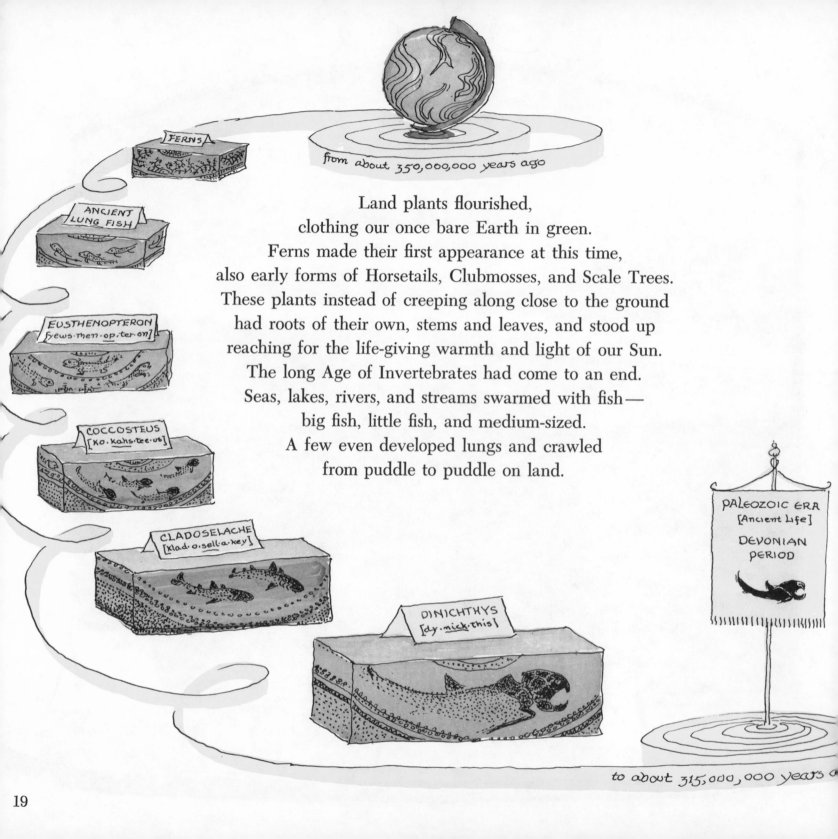

FERNS

ANCIENT LUNG FISH

EUSTHENOPTERON
[yews·then·op·ter·on]

COCCOSTEUS
[ko·kahs·tee·us]

CLADOSELACHE
[klad·o·sell·a·key]

DINICHTHYS
[dy·nick·this]

from about 350,000,000 years ago

Land plants flourished,
clothing our once bare Earth in green.
Ferns made their first appearance at this time,
also early forms of Horsetails, Clubmosses, and Scale Trees.
These plants instead of creeping along close to the ground
had roots of their own, stems and leaves, and stood up
reaching for the life-giving warmth and light of our Sun.
The long Age of Invertebrates had come to an end.
Seas, lakes, rivers, and streams swarmed with fish—
big fish, little fish, and medium-sized.
A few even developed lungs and crawled
from puddle to puddle on land.

PALEOZOIC ERA
[Ancient Life]

DEVONIAN
PERIOD

to about 315,000,000 years a

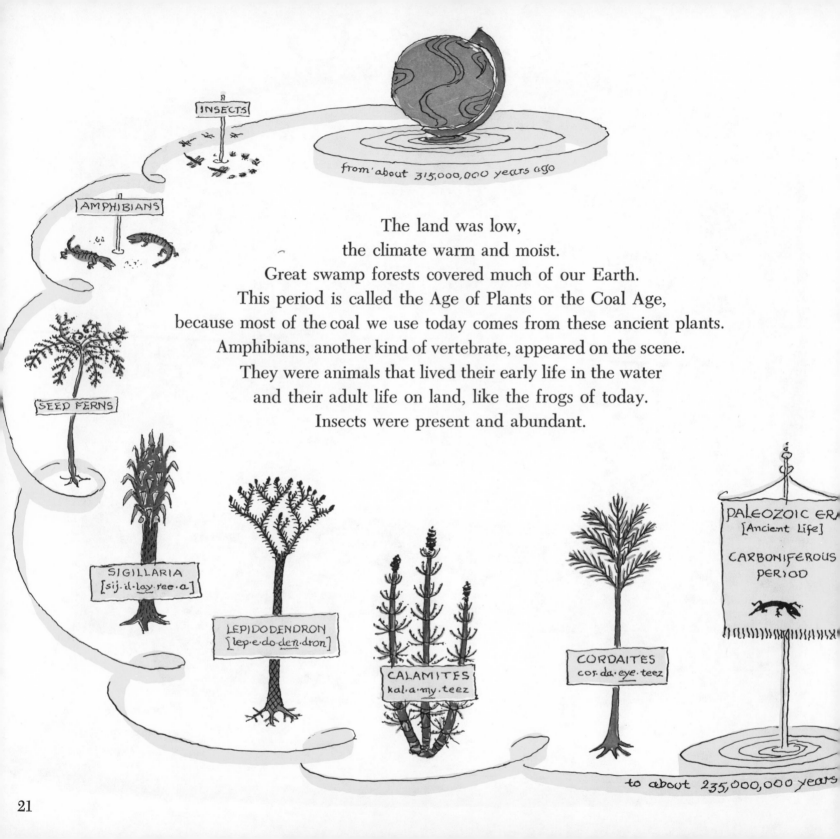

INSECTS

from about 315,000,000 years ago

AMPHIBIANS

SEED FERNS

The land was low,
the climate warm and moist.
Great swamp forests covered much of our Earth.
This period is called the Age of Plants or the Coal Age,
because most of the coal we use today comes from these ancient plants.
Amphibians, another kind of vertebrate, appeared on the scene.
They were animals that lived their early life in the water
and their adult life on land, like the frogs of today.
Insects were present and abundant.

SIGILLARIA
[sij·il·lay·ree·a]

LEPIDODENDRON
[lep·e·do·den·dron]

CALAMITES
kal·a·my·teez

CORDAITES
cor·da·eye·teez

PALEOZOIC ERA
[Ancient Life]

CARBONIFEROUS
PERIOD

to about 235,000,000 years

21

ACT
I

Scene 5

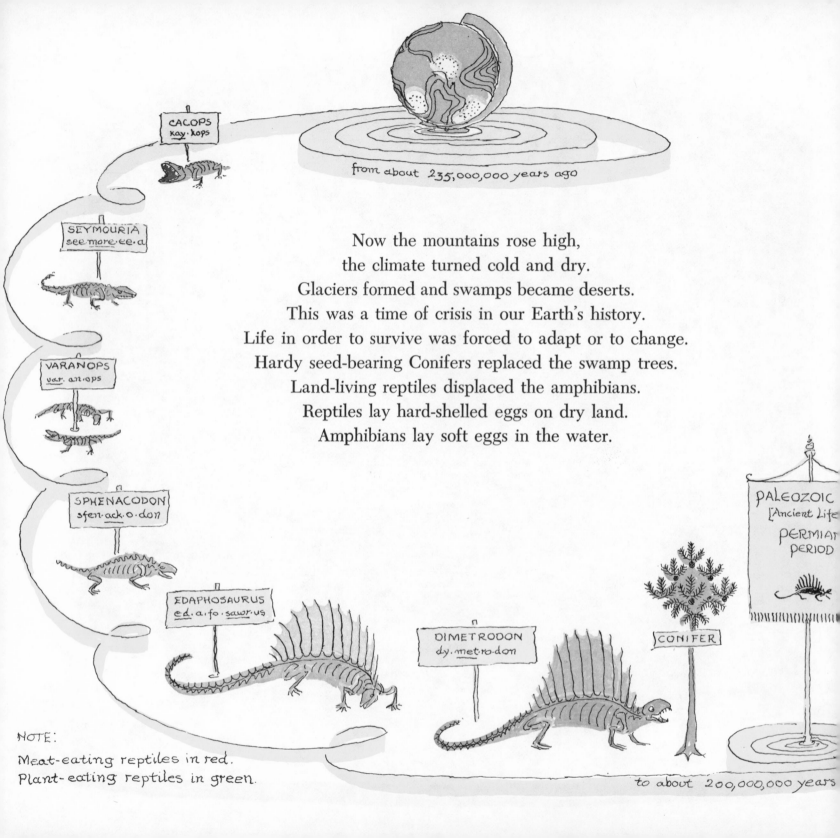

CACOPS
kay·kops

from about 235,000,000 years ago

SEYMOURIA
see·more·ee·a

VARANOPS
var·an·ops

Now the mountains rose high,
the climate turned cold and dry.
Glaciers formed and swamps became deserts.
This was a time of crisis in our Earth's history.
Life in order to survive was forced to adapt or to change.
Hardy seed-bearing Conifers replaced the swamp trees.
Land-living reptiles displaced the amphibians.
Reptiles lay hard-shelled eggs on dry land.
Amphibians lay soft eggs in the water.

SPHENACODON
sfen·ack·o·don

PALEOZOIC
[Ancient Life]
PERMIAN
PERIOD

EDAPHOSAURUS
ed·a·fo·sawr·us

DIMETRODON
dy·met·ro·don

CONIFER

NOTE:
Meat-eating reptiles in red.
Plant-eating reptiles in green.

to about 200,000,000 years

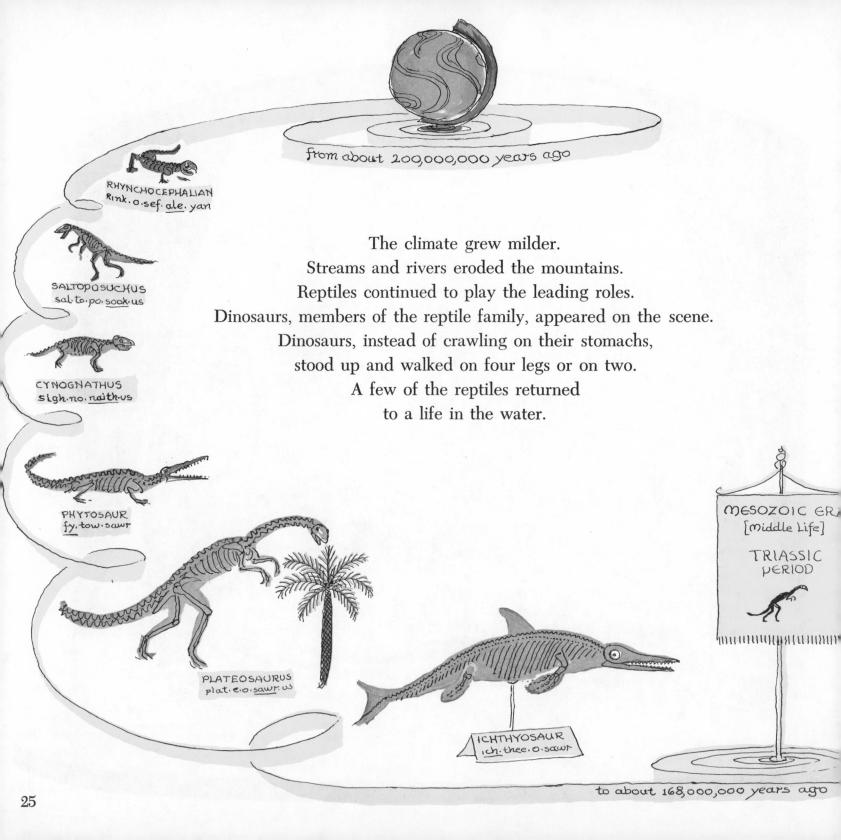

From about 200,000,000 years ago

RHYNCHOCEPHALIAN
Rink·o·sef·ale·yan

SALTOPOSUCHUS
sal·to·po·sook·us

CYNOGNATHUS
sigh·no·naith·us

PHYTOSAUR
fy·tow·sawr

PLATEOSAURUS
plat·e·o·sawr·us

ICHTHYOSAUR
ich·thee·o·sawr

The climate grew milder.
Streams and rivers eroded the mountains.
Reptiles continued to play the leading roles.
Dinosaurs, members of the reptile family, appeared on the scene.
Dinosaurs, instead of crawling on their stomachs,
stood up and walked on four legs or on two.
A few of the reptiles returned
to a life in the water.

MESOZOIC ERA
[Middle Life]

TRIASSIC
PERIOD

to about 168,000,000 years ago

25

ACT
II

Scene 1

from about 168,000,000 years ago

ANCIENT MAMMALS

ANCIENT BIRD

RHAMPHORYNCHUS
ram·for·<u>ink</u>·us

ORNITHOLESTES
or·<u>nith</u>·o·les·teez

Once again the climate was warm and moist.
Some of the plant-eating dinosaurs had grown tremendous.
Some had developed armor for protection from their meat-eating cousins.
Some reptiles had learned how to fly. The first real bird appeared.
Little mammals were present but they played
a very small part at this time.

ALLOSAURUS
al·o·<u>sawr</u>·us

BRONTOSAURUS
bron·to·<u>sawr</u>·us

STEGOSAURUS
steg·o·<u>sawr</u>·us

MESOZOIC ERA
[Middle Life]

JURASSIC
PERIOD

27

to about 130,000,000 years ago

ACT
II

SCENE 2

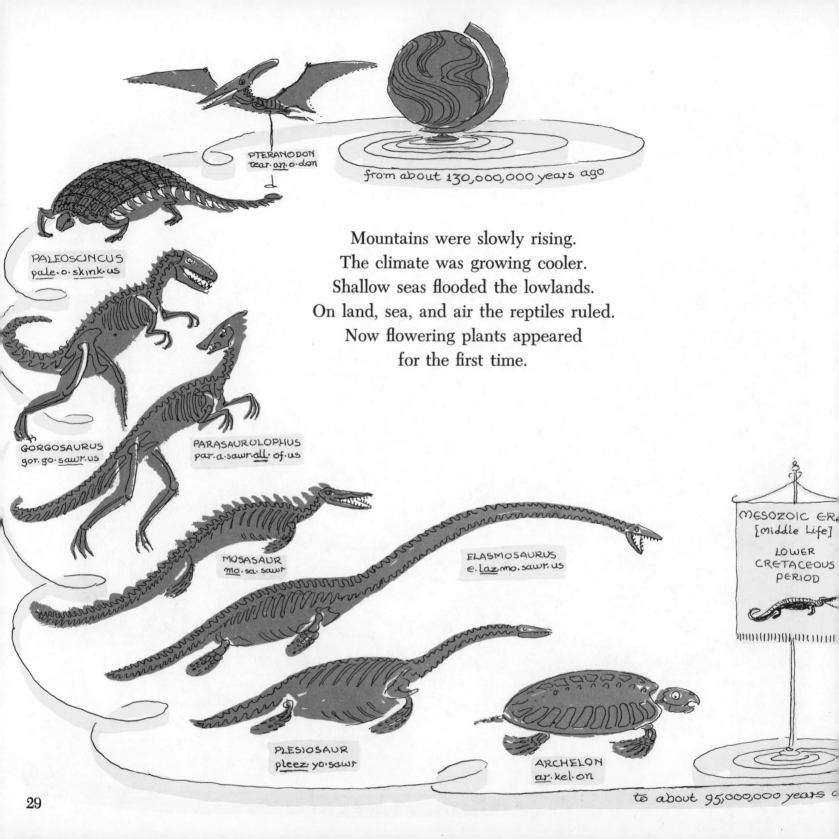

PTERANODON
tear·an·o·don

from about 130,000,000 years ago

PALEOSCINCUS
pale·o·skink·us

Mountains were slowly rising.
The climate was growing cooler.
Shallow seas flooded the lowlands.
On land, sea, and air the reptiles ruled.
Now flowering plants appeared
for the first time.

GORGOSAURUS
gor·go·sawr·us

PARASAUROLOPHUS
par·a·sawr·all·of·us

MOSASAUR
mo·sa·sawr

ELASMOSAURUS
e·laz·mo·sawr·us

MESOZOIC ERA
[Middle Life]

LOWER
CRETACEOUS
PERIOD

PLESIOSAUR
pleez·yo·sawr

ARCHELON
ar·kel·on

to about 95,000,000 years a

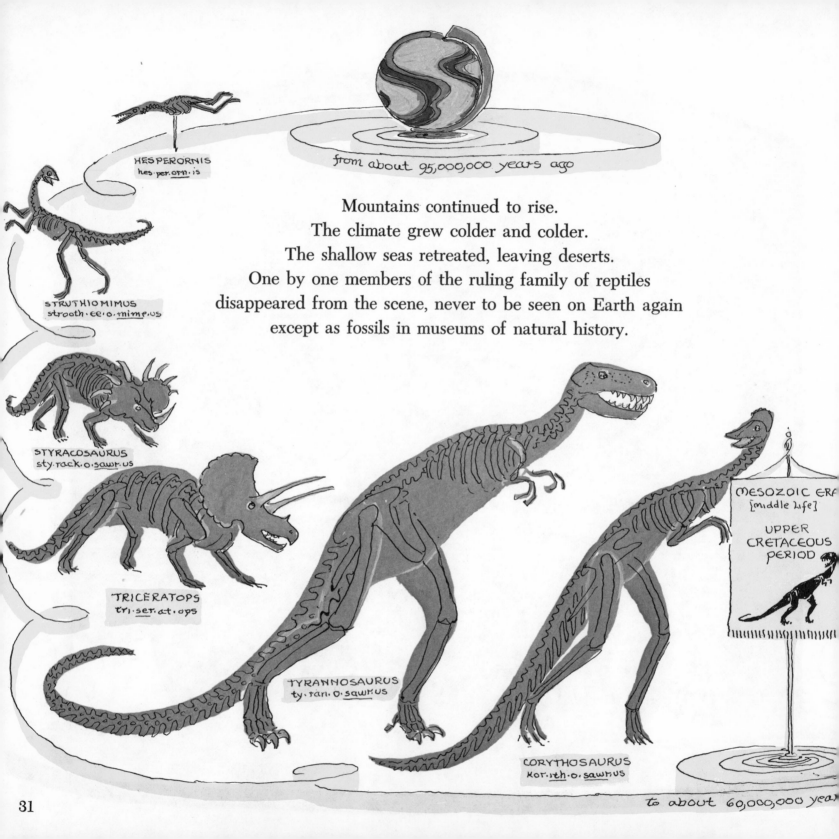

from about 95,000,000 years ago

HESPERORNIS
hes·per·orn·is

STRUTHIOMIMUS
strooth·ee·o·mime·us

Mountains continued to rise.
The climate grew colder and colder.
The shallow seas retreated, leaving deserts.
One by one members of the ruling family of reptiles
disappeared from the scene, never to be seen on Earth again
except as fossils in museums of natural history.

STYRACOSAURUS
sty·rack·o·sawr·us

TRICERATOPS
tri·ser·at·ops

TYRANNOSAURUS
ty·ran·o·sawr·us

CORYTHOSAURUS
kor·ith·o·sawr·us

MESOZOIC ERA
[middle life]

UPPER
CRETACEOUS
PERIOD

to about 60,000,000 years

ACT
II

Scene 4

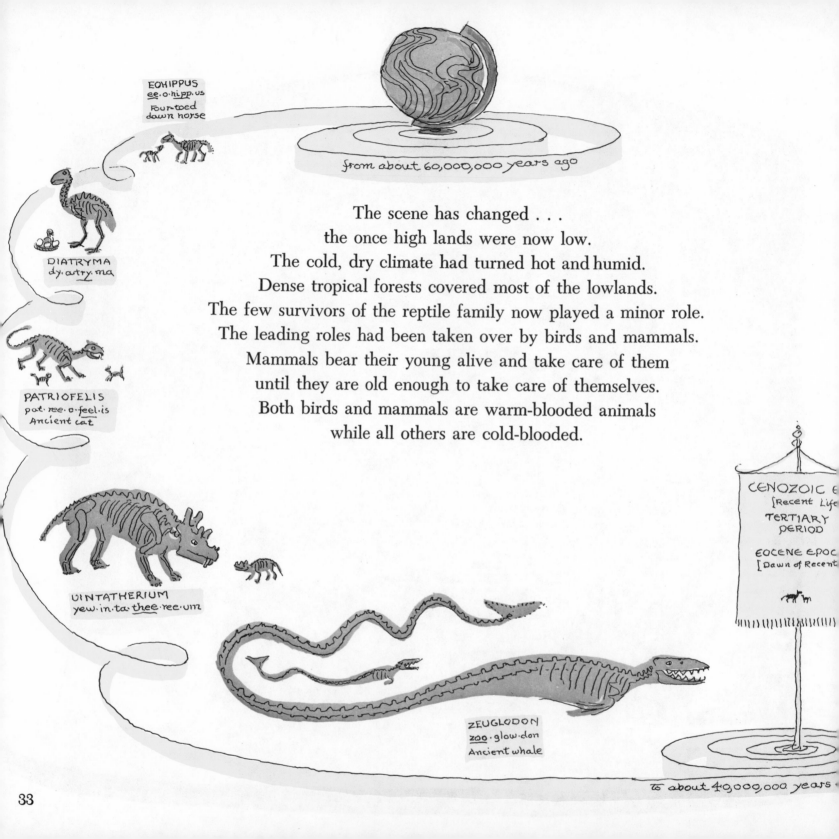

EOHIPPUS
ee·o·hipp·us
Four-toed
dawn horse

from about 60,000,000 years ago

DIATRYMA
dy·a·try·ma

PATRIOFELIS
pat·ree·o·feel·is
Ancient cat

The scene has changed . . .
the once high lands were now low.
The cold, dry climate had turned hot and humid.
Dense tropical forests covered most of the lowlands.
The few survivors of the reptile family now played a minor role.
The leading roles had been taken over by birds and mammals.
Mammals bear their young alive and take care of them
until they are old enough to take care of themselves.
Both birds and mammals are warm-blooded animals
while all others are cold-blooded.

UINTATHERIUM
yew·in·ta·thee·ree·um

CENOZOIC E
[Recent Life
TERTIARY
PERIOD

EOCENE EPOC
[Dawn of Recent

ZEUGLODON
zoo·glow·don
Ancient whale

to about 40,000,000 years

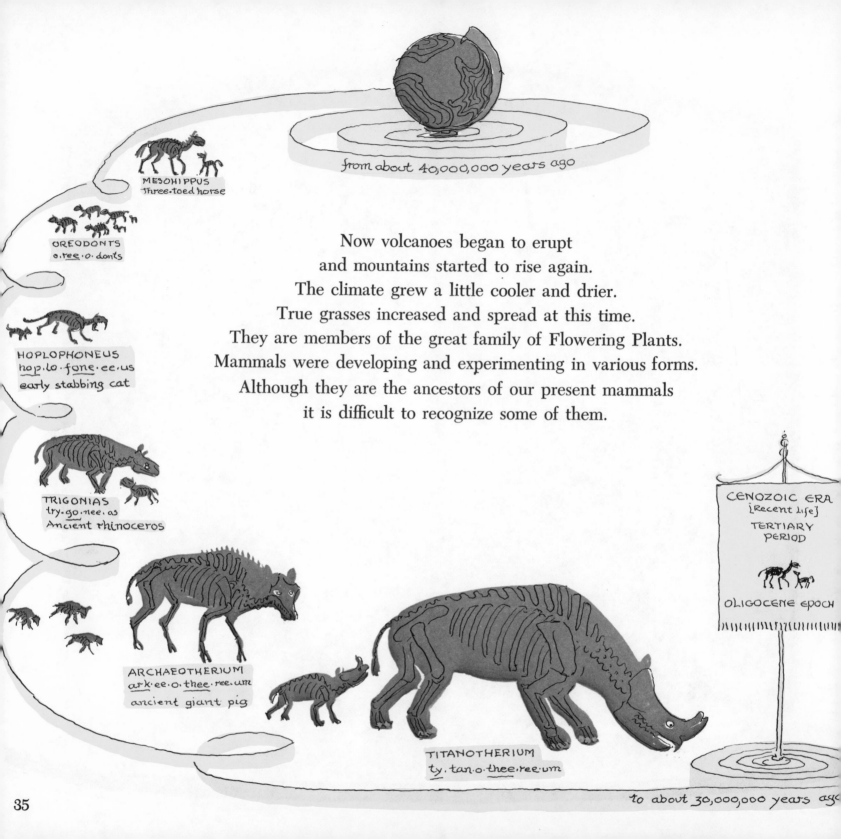

from about 40,000,000 years ago

MESOHIPPUS
Three-toed horse

OREODONTS
o·ree·o·donts

HOPLOPHONEUS
hop·lo·fone·ee·us
early stabbing cat

TRIGONIAS
try·go·nee·as
Ancient rhinoceros

ARCHAEOTHERIUM
ark·ee·o·thee·ree·um
ancient giant pig

TITANOTHERIUM
ty·tan·o·thee·ree·um

Now volcanoes began to erupt
and mountains started to rise again.
The climate grew a little cooler and drier.
True grasses increased and spread at this time.
They are members of the great family of Flowering Plants.
Mammals were developing and experimenting in various forms.
Although they are the ancestors of our present mammals
it is difficult to recognize some of them.

CENOZOIC ERA
[Recent Life]

TERTIARY
PERIOD

OLIGOCENE EPOCH

to about 30,000,000 years ago

ACT
III

Scene 2

from about 30,000,000 years ago

SYNDYOCERAS
sin·di·os·er·as

MERYCHIPPUS
mer·i·kip·us
a grazing horse

DINOHYUS
dy·no·hy·us
a piglike animal

MOROPUS
more·o·pus

ALTICAMELUS
all·tee·ka·mee·lus
ancient giraffelike camel

BALUCHITHERIUM
ba·luke·e·thee·ree·um
largest land mammal

Mountains continued to rise
and volcanoes continued to erupt.
The climate grew steadily cooler and drier.
Grasses spread rapidly making open plains instead of forests.
Plant-eaters changed their diet of leaves to one of grass.
The rule of the mammals was now at its height.
A few of them grew very big and tall—
the largest land mammals
of all time.

CENOZOIC ERA
[Recent Life]

TERTIARY
PERIOD

MIOCENE EPOCH

to about 12,000,000 years ago

SABER-TOOTH CAT

from about 12,000,000 years ago

PLIOHIPPUS
one toed horse

Volcanoes and mountain building
had reached their climax at this time.
The climate had grown exceedingly cold and dry.
Life was very difficult for the plants and animals.
Grasses had dried up and the plains were now deserts.
Earlier forms of mammals had become extinct.
The surviving forms now looked more like
the mammals we know today.

SYNTHETOCERAS
sin·the·toe·sair·as

CAMEL

RHINOCEROS

ANCIENT ELEPHANT

CENOZOIC ERA
[Recent Life]

TERTIARY
PERIOD

PLIOCENE EPOCH

To about 1,000,000 years

from about 1,000,000 years ago

TERATORNIS
a monstrous bird

ICE AGE HORSE

ICE AGE LION

In the north great glaciers formed
and slowly moved southward, scraping the land bare.
This time in Life's history on Earth is called the Ice Age.
Four times these great masses of ice advanced
and four times they melted and retreated.
Man was most probably present at this time
but he played a very minor role.

WOOLLY RHINOCEROS

GIANT CAMEL

WOOLLY MAMMOTH

CENOZOIC ER
[Recent Life]

QUATERNARY
PERIOD

PLEISTOCENE EPOC

to about 25,000 ? years ago

ACT
III
Scene 5

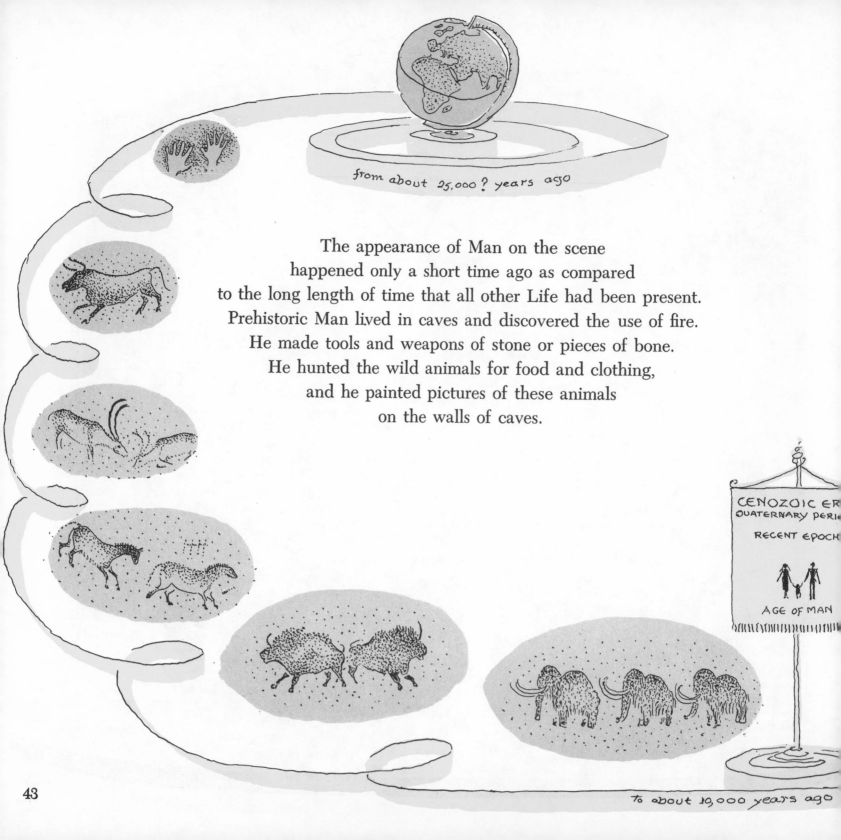

from about 25,000 ? years ago

The appearance of Man on the scene
happened only a short time ago as compared
to the long length of time that all other Life had been present.
Prehistoric Man lived in caves and discovered the use of fire.
He made tools and weapons of stone or pieces of bone.
He hunted the wild animals for food and clothing,
and he painted pictures of these animals
on the walls of caves.

CENOZOIC ERA
QUATERNARY PERIOD

RECENT EPOCH

AGE OF MAN

to about 10,000 years ago

ACT
IV

Scene 1

from about 10,000 years ago

Man learned how to cultivate plants
and domesticate animals for his own use.
Instead of wandering around and living in caves
he built houses and lived in villages, towns, and cities.
He found out how to build boats and to sail the high seas.
With the development of languages, recorded history began.
Historians tell the story of the rise and fall
of the great civilizations of the Old World
and the discovery of the New World.

to about 350 years ago

ACT
IV

Scene 2

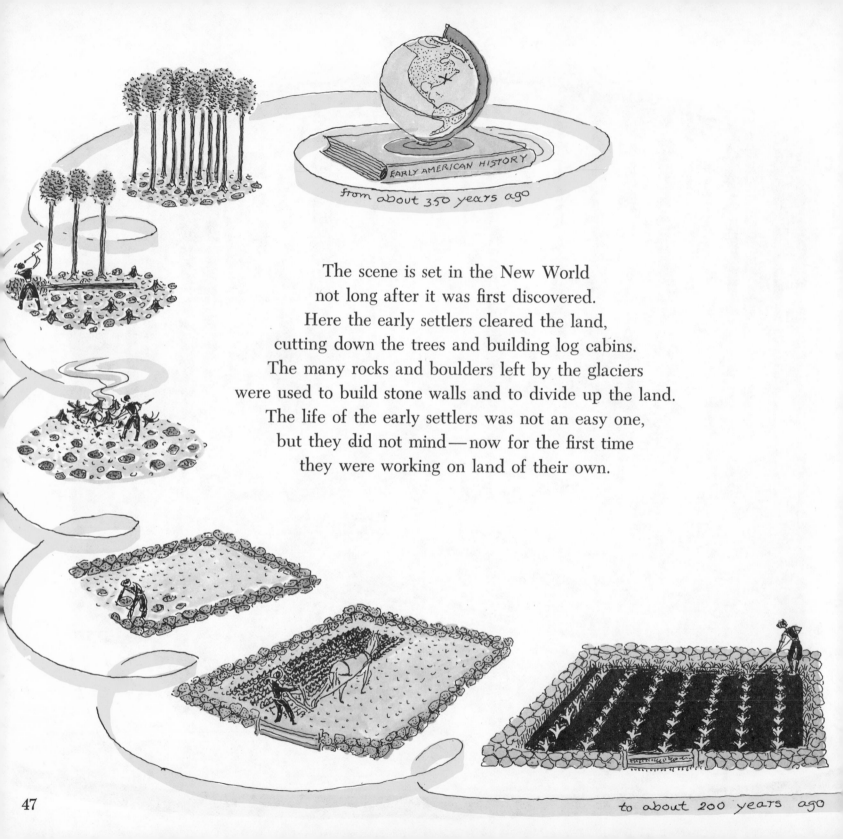

from about 350 years ago

The scene is set in the New World
not long after it was first discovered.
Here the early settlers cleared the land,
cutting down the trees and building log cabins.
The many rocks and boulders left by the glaciers
were used to build stone walls and to divide up the land.
The life of the early settlers was not an easy one,
but they did not mind—now for the first time
they were working on land of their own.

to about 200 years ago

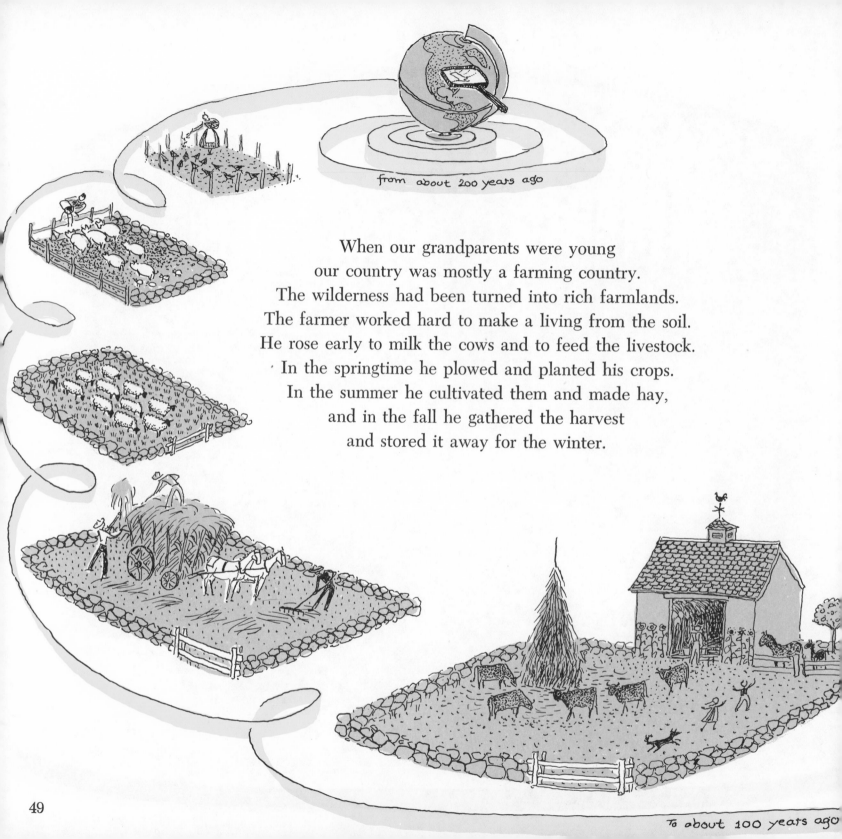

from about 200 years ago

When our grandparents were young
our country was mostly a farming country.
The wilderness had been turned into rich farmlands.
The farmer worked hard to make a living from the soil.
He rose early to milk the cows and to feed the livestock.
In the springtime he plowed and planted his crops.
In the summer he cultivated them and made hay,
and in the fall he gathered the harvest
and stored it away for the winter.

To about 100 years ago

ACT
IV

Scene 4

from about a 100 years ago

And now, a few generations later,
the once well-cared-for farms were deserted.
The farmers had either gone West or moved into the cities.
The fields were overgrown with briers, bushes, and trees.
All that remained to show that Man had lived here
were the stone walls dividing the land
and a few old apple trees.

51

to about 25 years ago

from about 25 years ago

Twenty-five summers have passed quickly
since we bought the old orchard, meadow, and woodland
and moved a little house and my barn studio into the middle of it.
The old apple trees have been trimmed, the woods cleaned up,
and in the meadow we have put sheep to keep the grass down.
Evergreens and flowering plants have been planted.
Ferns and mosses grow by the running brook.
Here is where we raised our children
until they grew old enough to begin
living a life of their own.

to about a year ago

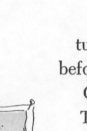

The season has changed from summer to fall.
The days are shorter and the nights are longer.
The air is cooler and the first frost nips the plants,
turning the green leaves to bright red, orange, and yellow
before they are caught by the wind and flutter to the ground.
Only the hardy evergreens are not affected by the cold.
The sap in the trees and shrubs sinks low in the roots—
and the seeds for next year's plants have been shed.
Many birds fly south to escape the winter.

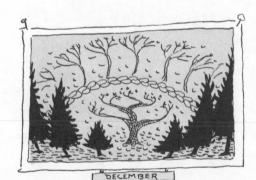

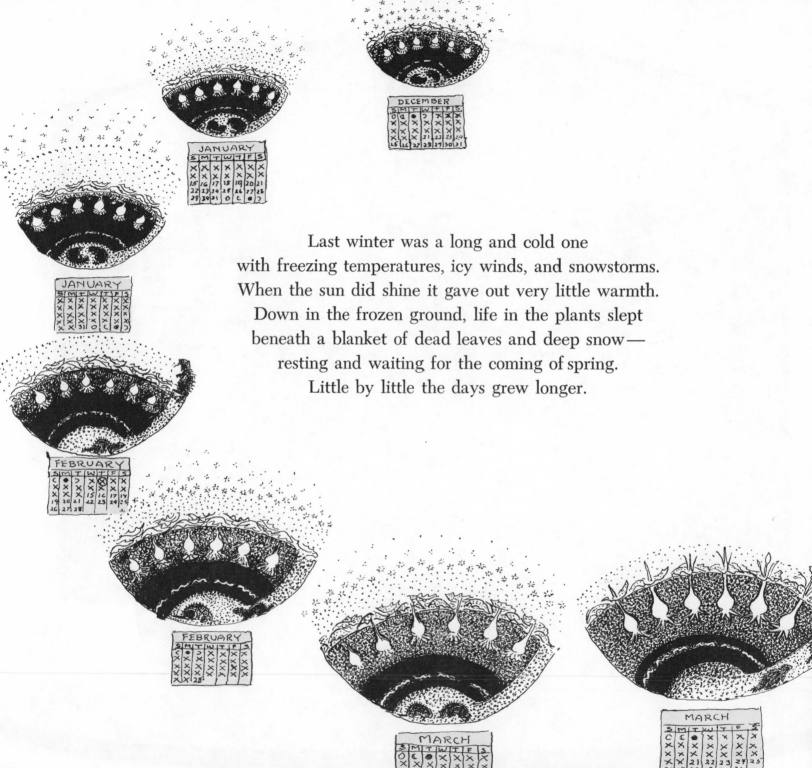

Last winter was a long and cold one
with freezing temperatures, icy winds, and snowstorms.
When the sun did shine it gave out very little warmth.
Down in the frozen ground, life in the plants slept
beneath a blanket of dead leaves and deep snow—
resting and waiting for the coming of spring.
Little by little the days grew longer.

In the first month of spring
the snow melted and the ground thawed.
Day by day, week by week the grass grew greener.
Gentle showers encouraged the early spring flowers.
In the trees the sap was rising, swelling the new buds.
Under the ground last year's seeds began to stir and awaken,
pushing tender shoots up through the earth and dead leaves,
reaching up for the light and warmth of the sun.
The birds returned from the South.

Yesterday was a day to remember—
one of those beautiful warm spring days
when one could almost see the plants growing.
Lowly little lichens clinging to the rocks brightened,
liverworts and velvety mosses carpeted the damp ground,
ferns pushed up and unfurled their delicate fronds,
new bright green needles tipped the evergreens,
buds opened and tiny little leaves unfolded,
and the apple trees burst into blossom.
In the meadow the sheep grazed happily
on the tender new shoots of grass.
The miracle of spring was here.

ACT
V

Scene 5

As the afternoon hours slipped by
and the sun began to sink in the west,
the shadows on the ground gradually lengthened.
Just before the sun set it turned fiery red,
tinting the sky and the earth bright pink.
High overhead a pale new moon appeared.
By the brook the frogs were singing
their song of spring.

The new moon had set
and darkness had fallen.
One by one the stars had come out—
millions and billions of stars, trillions of miles away.
The Big Dipper hung high in the bright spring sky
pointing out the steady-standing North Star.
Low on the horizon gleamed the Milky Way.
Inside the house the hands of the clock
showed that another day had passed
and a new day had begun.

ACT
V
Scene 7

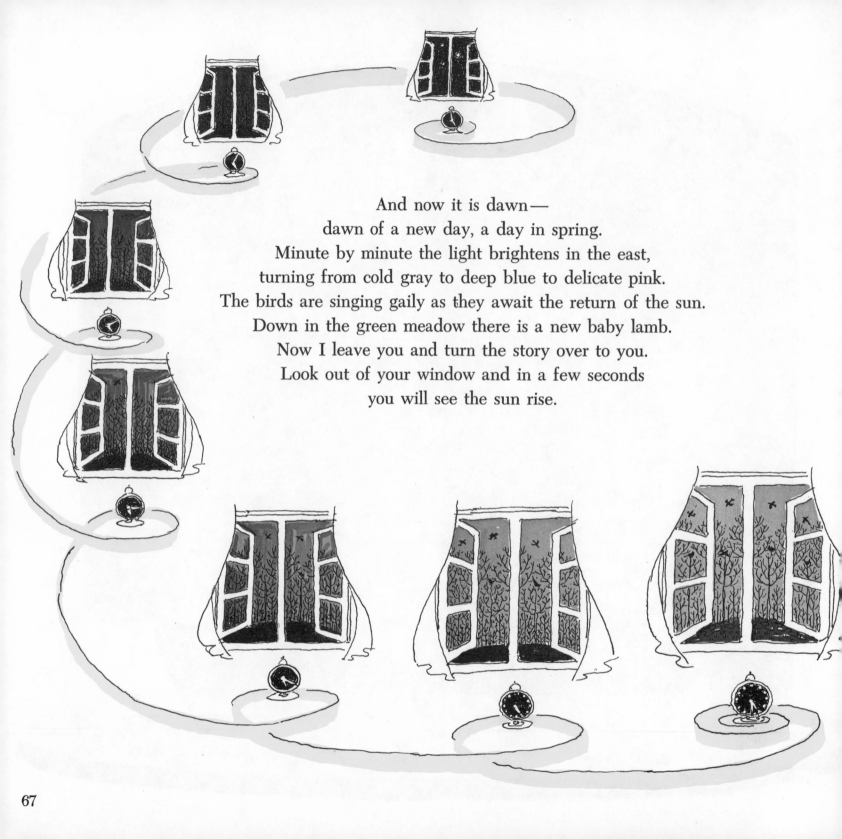

And now it is dawn—
dawn of a new day, a day in spring.
Minute by minute the light brightens in the east,
turning from cold gray to deep blue to delicate pink.
The birds are singing gaily as they await the return of the sun.
Down in the green meadow there is a new baby lamb.
Now I leave you and turn the story over to you.
Look out of your window and in a few seconds
you will see the sun rise.

ACT
V

Scene 8

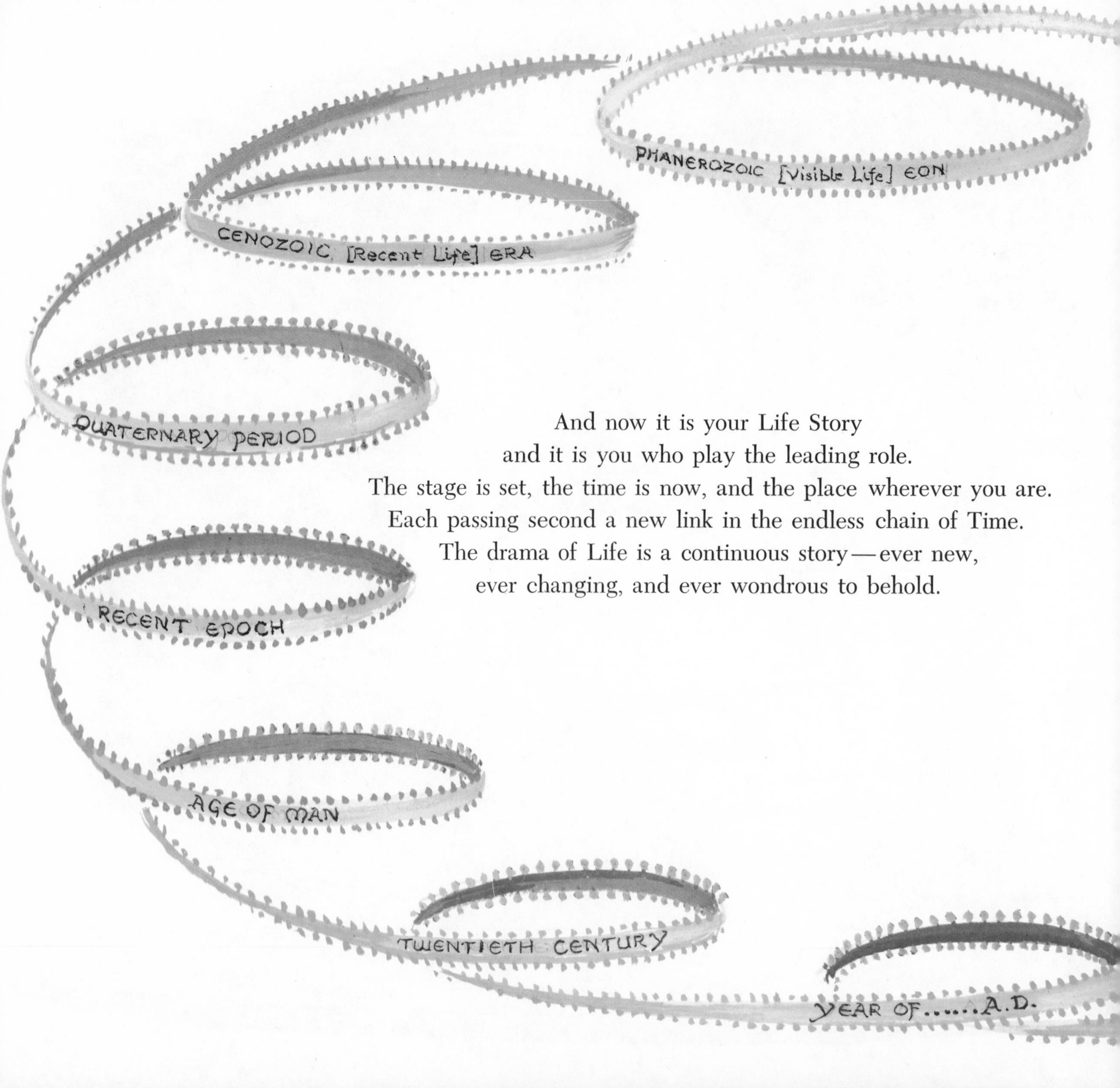

PHANEROZOIC [Visible Life] EON

CENOZOIC [Recent Life] ERA

QUATERNARY PERIOD

RECENT EPOCH

AGE OF MAN

And now it is your Life Story
and it is you who play the leading role.
The stage is set, the time is now, and the place wherever you are.
Each passing second a new link in the endless chain of Time.
The drama of Life is a continuous story—ever new,
ever changing, and ever wondrous to behold.

TWENTIETH CENTURY

YEAR OF......A.D.

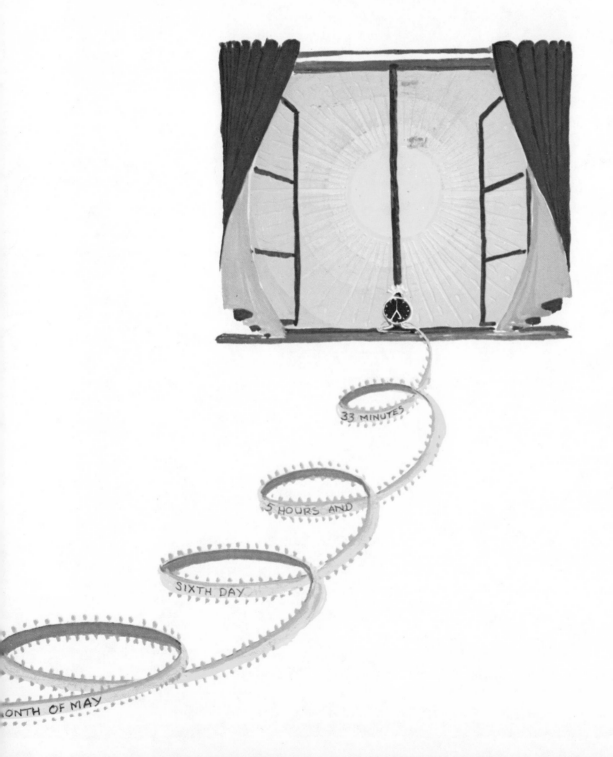

MAMMALS BIRDS REPTILES AMPHIBIANS FISH

PROTOZOA SPONGES COELENTERATA WORMS ECHINODERMS MOLLUSCS ARTHROPODS

FLOWERING PLANTS CONIFERS FERNS MOSSES ALGAE FUNGI BACTERIA

LICHEN

MUSE
OF
NATU
HISTO

IGNEOUS ROCKS METAMORPHIC ROCKS SEDIMENTARY ROCKS

To MUSEUM

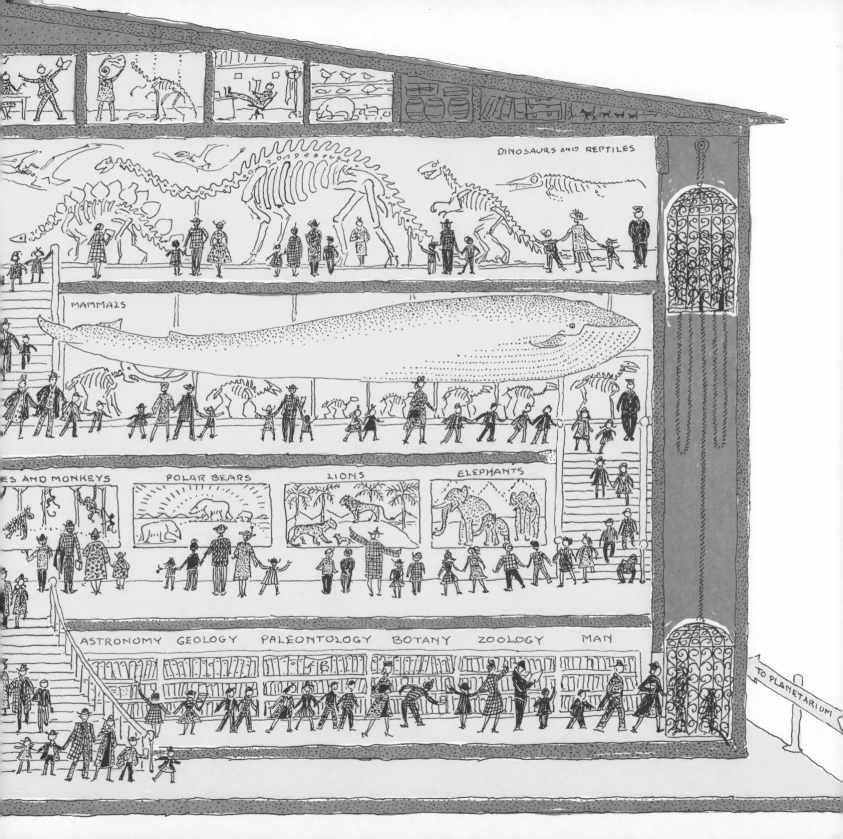

DINOSAURS AND REPTILES

MAMMALS

ES AND MONKEYS   POLAR BEARS   LIONS   ELEPHANTS

ASTRONOMY GEOLOGY PALEONTOLOGY BOTANY ZOOLOGY MAN

TO PLANETARIUM